Manifestations

Rucha Arun Shete

BookLeaf Publishing

Presentation by *BookLeaf Publishing*

Web: www.bookleafpub.com

E-mail: info@bookleafpub.com

ISBN: 978-93-5774-130-9

First edition 2023

Disclaimer

This book is made with utmost love of all the poems written in context in that phase of my life.

Please give it love by reading and hopefully relating to some of the poems.

Any resemblance to any of the feelings from the poem felt by you in any event of your life is completely a coincidence.

Please read and while reading think of a title for the poem.

To make you think all the poems have titles at the bottom.

Enjoy with creativity!!!

Rantings of the beautiful mind

I want those words
That tell me I deserve it
I want to hear those words
That thank me for the efforts I put in
I want to hear those words
That tell me I can achieve what I want
That it will be worth it
The risks that I put in
The struggles that I go through
Just don't leave the playground
The applause that you hear is not just a
sound
Its your dream your motivation
To help you get on and move ahead
There is no looking back now
There is no looking back now
There is no looking back now!

Self-validation!!

This is no time to laugh at others faults
But to stand by them help them, that's what
our mothers taught
The storm will come and then go
After all this will you even recognize your
foe
Storm makes us realize what is essential
Hardwork, trust, faith, honesty, yes that
works
Patience, patience, patience and patience is
tried by us
Here and there, this and that – No time to
make a fuss
Not able to go out, so what Look inside
You will be seriously amazed at what you
will find
Selfish needs are long being forgotten now
Always for the greater good we shall strive
towards, we know how!

From a Covid warrior!!

I have always wanted to be normal
But that was just a way to be formal
Happiness I seek always
Is it normal Is a question I raise
Too much happiness is mania
Don't want to be insane or crazier
Never Never Never been normal I say
Lets all for content and acceptance pray!

#neverbeenormal

I am missing going out for a walk
Always there would be someone with whom
I would stop and talk
I miss going to Juhu beach
Sitting on the sand looking at the waves just
out of reach
I don't miss travelling in local trains
The hurry the crowd not wanting especially
in the rains
I miss the mountains and the rivers
Sitting on the grass staring at sunset not
caring about little creatures
Oh! the friends, their talks
Eating outside, dancing making me not
glance at the clocks
But I have time to make plans
Working for the greater good and not just
glam
Gives me strength courage and a will
Lots to do later, patience I will keep

Lockdown musings

FREEDOM

When a person wants to commit suicide
Its not a weakness, a get away
But the only option at that time
Life can be beautiful again
Tell them and make them stay
Let them struggle to make it through
Just give support and stand by their blues

Options

Happy to be sad
Sad to be Happy

What are the odds?
That a guy like you
Would hang out with
A girl like me!
The guy ???
Oh He is famous, a social butterfly
Me???
I am awkward I just comply
He was something I wanted to be
Self-righteous, confident perfect and Free
He looked good according to the standards
I just tried hard, honesty was my beauty
card
I thought this was just part of school
But No
Outside world also is filled with fools

Comparisons

A privilege to do something later
It must be laziness
Or just disorganized craziness
The to do list is taped to the wall
But humpty Dumpty had a great fall
St Kabir wants you to do everything now
only
But you just want to laze and breathe slowly
Whats the hurry you say
Still you complete it last minute and pray
Pray pray and Hope that
Job done is better even though not perfect at
all!!

Love

What is right? What is wrong?
What makes the words into a song?
Everybody lies and that is the truth
Why do we always want the forbidden fruit?
They stand by you. But you are alone
What you do cannot be even done by your
clone
You write what you feel is the best story for
you
Otherwise somebody else will write it for
you

Take care

Hello HI How are you?
They matter even though few
The conversation Starts
Noone knows how long it lasts
Minutes, Hours Days Years
The "Samvad" removes all fears
1 step 1 day at a time
Don't be surprised when you say "I am Fine"

Greetings

Seemed an easy task
You just had to find the guts to ask
Whether I would be enough was always the
fear
But who was meant for whom?
No one could tell not even the seer
We meet one and then another and then so
many
Is it that hard to start a family?
Then you get used to it the novelty worn off
Why do people marry?
Just so people don't scoff
May be love was meant to be only for
oneself
The longing the feelings pack it and keep it
in that shelf
Loving yourself is equal to loving everyone
Then you will realize it is not a burden but
lots of fun!

Finding Love

Dream catchers
Grow Big dreams, have a purpose they say
What about the small dreams?
Which everyday at night play
And the day dreaming that gives hope
But keeps the present from happening
Do we ignore?
Are they not important?
YES they are
But you don't want to be labelled as an
escapist
Hold on to them, don't let them go
They will give you ideas to go against the
flow
Stay strong let them follow you
Make the world a better place for them and
you!!!

Dream catchers

To the girl who didn't believe in herself
Who was she in the grand scheme of things
Envious of people around her
All the smartness she knew she deserved
Being honest she couldn't fake it
Till finally she did make it
Making it for herself for nothing was more
important than being content to her
Connecting people spreading the happiness
pandemic
Like she used to be, her teenage self
Focused on the next immediate task and not
worrying about the bigger goals
One day at a time she followed
Little did she know that each drop she added
did make an ocean
An ocean where everyone was included and
not judged
An ocean where people felt safe and
understood
Knew that here their secrets would be kept
safe
And if they were discussed it would not only
help them but also others to grow at last
So the pandemic is still ongoing

But this time to be honest you will have to
take off your masks

To the girl who knew nothing

EPIDEMIOLOGY AND
MANAGEMENT FOR HEALTH CARE

I see the river flowing and the mountains
watching
Do the mountains mock the river and keep
judging ?
The river dances sings and flounces
It wants the mountains approval as on the
rocks it bounces
It's proud of its fluidity and wants to prove
those age old mountains wrong
The river is as fresh as it can be converting
everything into a song
The river calls it self love and mocks the
mountains to b so hard on themselves
Averting the eyes of the mountains it also
shows it strength and toughness
It helps the earth grow it can mould the
rocks and pebbles
It prevents draught and provides relief to
animals
What's the meaning of the lonely standing
mountain she laughs
Only when she reaches the ocean she
realises her origin, sees the mountain laugh.

peace

On the way
Swallow sitting on the telephone lines
Granite marble stores, trucks and signs
That tell me I am going where I need to
To do what was meant so
With the sun in my eyes, music in my ears
And a purpose I held for so many years
I go to the village, Raees bhai driving
I know there r people waiting
Wanting to tell me their stories
Their fears, doubts and worries
I hope along with the pill I give
They get something more, a will to live
And not just live but to live wholesome
As I have been taught
Taught not to earn the bread
But also to make the bread and give the
bread
To those who ask of it
Making the world a better place bit by bit!

On the way

The world I wished
Stepping out of the house on green grass
Fresh as a daisy, at the start of the day
Sun shining, passerby's smiling
Exchanging news that is nothing but
progress
Past all forgotten starting anew
Creating relationships not boundaries
Living for the self and to help those who
can't
Nothing left in whole wide world to rant
Peace, harmony, honesty
Can hear the birds chirping constantly
The greater good which was the purpose
you toiled for is here babe
There was nothing hard about the hard
work you did
Because it was inside you all along the way!

The world I wished

MAGIC

Flame of the forest
From afar it looks like a flame
You wouldn't wander near it, you scared
It's not everyday to see
A humble tree so fiery
Standing out in the plain
Showing off, but in vain
Beauty lies in the eye of the beholder
It is summer now but it will get colder
The flames are just flowers
Sore to the eyes together
But in all their uniqueness
You won't find anything else prettier!

To the universe
Simply put, carbon hydrogen and oxygen
Atoms molecules creating energy vibrations
Together making up a human who can feel
Not just feel but think about the feeling and
think about the thinking
How complicated!
Don't you get tired?
Putting all these together
Making sure it keeps continuing
History does repeat with it new pro versions
Some will keep creating wars and
distributing cynicism for free
While some maybe few will live carefree
Pure joy, free mind, not tied by strings
Don't get drunk on jealousy
These selfish people, unexpectedly giving
hope to all
Greater good they want
But for now just a hot mug of coffee, with a
good book and music will suffice!

To taking breaks
Give your mind a break
Constantly working,
Brain says Now don't stimulate
Don't brag about being in the hustle culture
Slowly patiently silently give yourself time
to nurture
Slow the pace
Stop the race
Cut the chase
Inhale and exhale
Listen to your heart, coz that's the universe
u have
At the beginning and at the start
So try to understand that first and then the
world out there last

My home
Like the feel of the soft carpet
On my naked scrubbed clean feet
Right after I get up from a dreamy sleep
Clean bed sheets, soft pillows
Carefully chosen Curtains swaying as the
wind blows
The mirror telling how I feel
As I brush my teeth
The macaroon mug I drink my coffee from
Caffeine energy in me making me feel I can
do all
I like my home because it's mine
The memory wall and the frames hanging
My home my space letting me be
Self love max that is infinite
No judgements no taunts filled with
positivity
Yes even though it's a strange city
But humans are humans
So I give them love the way I would want it

The space called home

Make a poem mind said
Feel the texture of words for which u cared.
Happy sad angry all emotions in the world
Understand them to put them on paper to be
sold
Once colourful the sheet was wiped clean
Nothing was der on it to be seen
One colour one emotion at a time
The coal had to go through the pressure,
later to shine
Things that were taken for granted became
a task.
Why d love of water became a fear i ask.
The journey is important not the goal
The things u learn can never be told
Once a delusion in mind
Similar but different of kind
Its a journey to make it true
Everyone will know now what you have
gone through.
Pick up the flower and smell it
This is the enjoyment u always need

**Once upon a time there was a
delusion**

The olfactory way
The stimulating caffeine smells
That wake u up
And your fruity shampoo flirts & tells
I am already yours just shut up
The new book is waiting
You open and take a deep breath
The koyal is singing
Reminding you of the foresty smells
Smell that take you to the mountains
Away from the concrete jungle
To be or not to be
Must not be the question
Because you don't have any options
Options only to choose
To heart or to dislike
They make you and break you
But you just long for the citrusy smell
From the orange orchards where they fell
Because The smells
They keep you in the present
They keep you in the present

The olfactory way

आमचं एक इवलसं पिल्लू
बघता बघता मोठं झालं
आपलं आगळं वेगळं पण
सगळ्यांना जाणवायला लागलं
कोठे चित्रकला तर कोठे लेखनकला
आणि त्यात भर म्हणून नृत्यकला
हसत हसत शिक्षणाची
सारी क्षेत्र पार करून
शिकता शिकता इतरांना शिकवत
ऊत्तिर्ण होऊन सर्वांना सुखवून
परदेशात आपला प्रबंध वाचून
सगळीकडे वाहवा मिळवून
आणि परत शोध घेतला
आपल्या दुर्लक्षित भागाचा
बंग पती पत्नींच्या शोधग्रामाचा
त्यांच्या छत्राखाली घेतला वसा आपल्या पुढच्या
आयुष्याच्या वाटचालीचा
खूप अभिमान वाटतो मला
माझ्या नातीचा

आबा

Blame game
It's easy to say your fault not mine
Easy to shirk and forgive say it's fine
Then you are the bigger person you feel
But to need someone and to accept that
makes your skin peel
You don't need anyone
You are invincible
But just for fun
Let's assume you are not capable
Not capable of facing your weakness
Not capable of admitting that in others
presence
Inside maybe you know what it is
Why it is
How it is
Learn to uplift people
Not downpull by being subtle
Honesty works and it's not to make yourself
inferior
But to help others feel they are also normal,
period.

Blame game

I feel the pain inside
It feels mine and only mine
The happiness that I get
Also mine, which I never forget
Why do I numb these feelings? to be
normal?
To feel is to live without which - red signal
I understand you but not in the same way
I understand myself, can't help but pray
Helping those who ask of it
And pray for those who don't
It's difficult to help myself but
Works when I help you
You who are a beautiful soul
A creation so unique that breathes
Only love can solve this
Love makes it easy
Doesn't come with instructions on how to
use it
Although the instructions are clear we blur
it
With hate jealousy ego sadness contempt
cynicism
Just take a duster and clean the slate
Use it as a mirror and you will know it's
never too late

Meta

Survival of the fittest
How can anyone be ignorant?
And be able to survive
But ignorance is bliss it is said
If you are honest you won't be caved
Hope for the future because
Past is already done and dusted
The present is all you have
If you appreciate you won't be busted
The restlessness will vanish
Only if you protect your heart from the fear
Fear that will tarnish
The image you created for yourself
And the world, no don't look at the shelf
Where you have kept those memories
To remember
Learning's, to help you survive
And not make the same mistakes
But bigger ones

Survival of the fittest

No not all boys are same
But when you have to select at random
You think they are
So the choice is difficult
I don't want a choice
Doesn't downtone my voice
Because all boys are the same
With the love they want and the love they
give
Sometimes going overboard
And sometimes oh the indifference
I have incorporated these qualities
Spending time with them at ease
They are warm category of humans
Sometimes pointless and aimless
But they care and only if you provoke
They might take you for granted
Give them respect and care
Only then u might get the same which is
rare
Learn to admire this rare entity
The supporting characters in our story
So to all the boys I have loved
Gratitude for breaking me making me and
for all those learning's I kept in my broken
heart

It wasn't easy to let go
But it is a must
Take it as another opportunity
to meet another entity

To all the boys I have loved

The name of the book is Manifestations. Since childhood I have been wanting things. Or rather I wanted my own life in a particular way. I do that today also. These poems are a small effort in my own way to putout into the universe what I want and manifest the same for myself.

Extremely grateful to you reader for going through the entire book!!
This book is meant to be scribbled and doodled upon.

www.ingramcontent.com/pod-product-compliance
Lightning Source LLC
La Vergne TN
LVHW010830200726
843508LV00012B/2546